And You Call Me The Pervert

Poems, Rants, & Artwork from Behind Prison Walls
From the Deviant Mind of Harry Hardcore

Written by:
Harry Hardcore

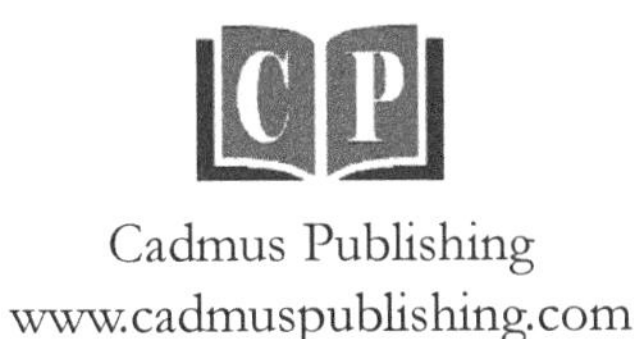

Cadmus Publishing
www.cadmuspublishing.com

Published by Cadmus Publishing
www.cadmuspublishing.com

ISBN: 978-1-63751-045-2

Foreword

Do you know what the problem is with most of you "normal" people? It's that through the sheer mass of your numbers, you get to navigate this life with the false perception that you are "RIGHT!"

Just by holding the opinions of the majority, you are allowed to perpetuate irrationalities, impose your will on those who are different, and walk around with an air of superiority - even though you don't know the "whys" behind your opinions. And you get to do all this while unashamed of your subjectivity and over-confident in your judgments.

Compared to the weight of your many voices, we who deviate from your social norms are but tiny moons, caught in your gravitational pull, forced to circle Uranus.

But if you were able to drop the arrogance of your certainty and had to be intellectually honest for once, you would see that promoting the absolutes of the majority is just a thinly-veiled version of the old medieval adage "Might Makes Right" - a saying you'd have never attributed to yourself on your own, and one that (had you been asked about before reading this) you would have certainly condemned as unenlightened and barbaric. But since it was a deviant like me who pointed out to you, you feel no shame for using it. After all, your righteous ends justify your means, don't they.

-That is a statement, not a question.-

As a person who spent his formative years concealing divergent opinions, I quietly watched from inside your circles, and I saw how you persecuted those who were reluctant to conform (in both overt and covert ways). And from this observation, I can say with confidence that the most damaging façade you perpetuate is that we are somehow vastly different from each other.

While my circadian rhythm may dictate that it's best for me to go to bed after midnight and rise around nine in the morning (instead of the ungodly five or six a.m. that you early-risers claim makes one "healthy, wealthy, and wise") that doesn't mean I lack character or need to be "corrected." I'm not evil-incarnate just because I don't believe that heterosexuality is the only natural/in-born sex drive, while all other variations are bad choices made by sick minds. (For Christ's sake, it's not like I'm one of those star-bellied Sneetches who should be eradicated by a eugenics program.)

But somehow all you normal people have come to the irrational conclusion that I can't possibly hold different views than you and be a good person. Granted, I'm locked up so I've definitely been a bad guy… but you seem to think that's *all* I am.

Look, I'm sure you are at least aware enough to realize that no one is single-dimensional; so why do you believe it's appropriate to demonize me entirely?

For decades I've worn a scarlet letter tattooed across my forehead, kicked like some dog begging for table scraps, shunned as if I were mono-chromatically evil. And for as long as I can remember, I've witnessed the glee in your eyes when you caused one of us perverts to fail.

You just love to whip out your majority gavel and bring it down on the heads of those who pollute your Wonder Bread® utopia.

By way of explanation, it's the horror of being on the receiving end of that gavel which has inspired me to publish my private thoughts and poetry. Perhaps through reading my words you will finally see that I have depth: That I am tender as well as harsh; that my heart is both beautiful as well as dark; and that I can be creative, insightful, and loving - as well as judgmental, crass, and criminal. That I, like you, am multifaceted.

In spite of the tough criticisms I've laid out here, I am actually looking for a way to heal our divisions, not punch you in the face for all the fear and bullying you've put me through.

And while I've proven that I'm not above lashing out in horrendous ways, my goal is not to take the gavel from you hand to use it on you, but to toss it in the trash so we can all stop being so tribal.

Now I know many of you mainstreamers believe that God told your group they are special, and provided y'all with exclusive access to Absolute Truth… But as long as that is your foundation, you'll always have (what to you is a reason, and to me is an excuse) to try and assimilate me. And this reveals what I'd bet is the biggest difference between you and me.

You see, I don't believe that my ideals, my traditions, and my ways of doing things are a blueprint of perfection - only that they're the best I've found so far. Therefore, I'm not driven to impose them upon you. Thus, my perception about what would heal the rifts between us is based upon making more tolerant spaces to accommodate everyone's variety. But your idea of healing consists only of converting me to your side.

You would ask me to change everything that makes me unique, when all I ask of you is that you stop shoving your opinions down my throat, telling me they are facts. I don't want to threaten your beliefs, I just want you to admit that belief is what they are.

Although I am truly sorry for the suffering I caused

my victims, I cannot apologize for being different than you. You'd never believe the amount of effort I put into trying to be part of your majority (in spite of the misery it caused me). And after decades of pondering this issue, I think it was the weight of that misery that I used to justify lashing out.

Sadly, it seems that if I could have found a way to be comfortable in my difference living among you mainstreamers, I think the probability of me becoming a criminal would have been much lower. But I have also concluded that is it human nature (not criminal nature) to violently resist being absorbed.

So read my rants and poems if you dare. Perhaps you will find proof that I'm nothing more than the iconoclast you believe me to be? Or perhaps you will find that I am more like you than is comfortable to admit?

In my experience, everyone is a pervert and/or deviant somewhere. The only reason you get to label and shame *me* is because my perverseness got exposed, and yours has yet to be.

After all, isn't your obsession with homogenizing everyone by force a perversion of the very freedom that built this country? Is that not a deviation from the freedom that enabled your ideals to become the majority?

And you call me the pervert?

Heart Blood

Inseparable as blood and life
The blade of the knife and the beating heart
For there cannot be love without risk
Meaningless without the fear of being torn apart
How can love be the greatest gift
Lest there be equal peril for its loss

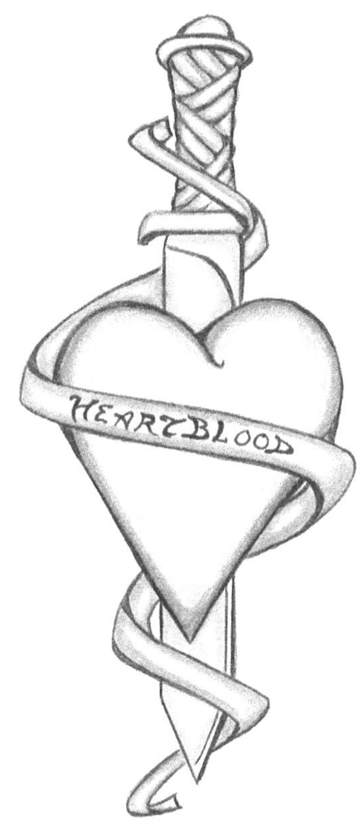

American Pride

We Hate, in the name of our Justice
We Punish, with unwavering Law
We Forgive, only those who deserve it
We Love, to watch people fall

Our Answers, are always the right ones
Our Beliefs, are God's absolute truth
Our Intentions, are beyond your reproach, so...
Our Conclusions, they need little proof

We Aspire, to out-do our neighbors
We Hope, to keep all of the pie
We Wish, that others were like us
We Have, so much you should buy

Our Sleep, is unburdened by conscience
Our Lives, are unclouded by doubt
Our Machine, will march onward undaunted
You don't like it? Then get the Hell Out!

Americans

We want to be right
More than we want to be loved.
We want to be rich
More than we want to be happy
And feared more than we want to be connected.

The Fool's Journal: Entry A-9: Worries

The Fool awakens in a panic, sweat streaming down his ashen face, his mind spinning. But his tortured dream has not ended, for there, sitting heavily upon his chest lies a demon… The Night Mare. And it laughs at the Fool's suffering.

"Your worries and fears have given me power over you" taunts the black and silky stallion, its eyes hot like gleeful embers.

"I gave you nothing!" the Fool screams back in desperation. "My fears exist because of my circumstances. I didn't fabricate them, they are real."

"And what do you gain by letting your thoughts run circles around your so-called circumstances?" responds the inky spirit. "I'll tell you what you gain and I speak true - for I am a demon of suffering, not of lies. All you gain from your worry is my presence. Because you are the author of your thoughts, it was you who invited me to sit on your chest."

"But what was, I cannot change," protests the Fool. "And over what might be, I have little control. Loss, sorrow, failure… all these and more have plagued my life - and will likely continue to do so. I am afraid because I cannot stop them."

"Perhaps not," smiled the demon. "But all I care about is that you keep feeding me all your delicious worries. And on top of all your 'real' problems, I will grow fat. Keep letting your mind run wild and soon my girth will blot out the sun. And when that occurs, fear and worry are all you will ever see again."

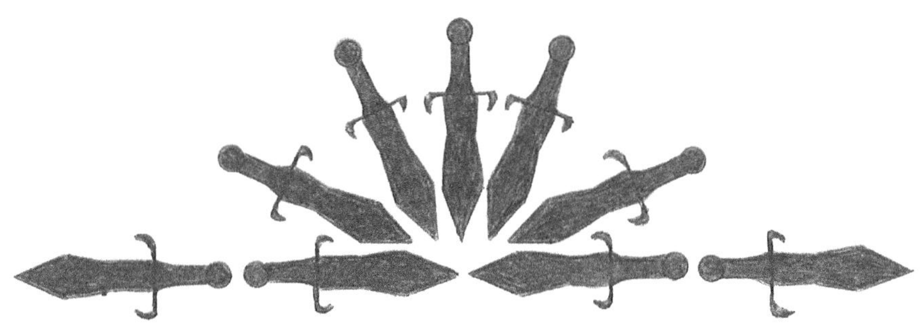

I NEVER TOLD YOU

In early morning's twilight, my dreams of you scatter
and my sleeping mind fumbles to hold on to
the arch of your back and the tangles of your hair
that are slipping away into another realm of consciousness.
Futile hopes of escaping the reality
of a far too noisy alarm clock.

A brush of my hand across my face revives your image;
as your scent still lingers on my skin and in the linen of my bed.
As I open my mouth I can still taste you on my lips.
Now, in place of dreams come memories:
Vivid,
and real,
and enchanting.

I wander through the city's streets,
and though the day is gray,
I do not feel the hint of cold, the drops of rain,
or the curses of those unfortunate enough to be driving next to
me in my distracted state of mind.
I only feel your hands running through my hair
and across my chest.

Once again I brush my hand across my face,
as I will do a hundred times today.
I inhale,
remember,
and smile.

The Price of Thinking

The peaceful silence of my mind
is broken by the words that form my thoughts.
What is this need I have to change my emotions
into crisscross lines that fill pages of white paper?
Staining them forever with toxic tints of blue and black.
Those words cloud the purity of my emotions,
much as this ink pollutes the page upon which I write.
Why should I taint my feelings with circular wording?
The pros, the cons, the perfect adjective, the correct spelling.
When I cannot put what I feel into words, I frustrate myself.
Thereby changing the feeling.
But I cannot let my emotions go undefined.
For in no way can they show me absolute rightness,
or wrongness.
And so I analyze...
and sacrifice my feelings for thoughts.

Sea Salt Shattered in a Wavebreak

Shadows cloak my mortal will.
They keep me warm in hiding but cold in living.
Time slips, memories fade, experience is my only savor.
All less fulfilling each time repeated.

Do I calm myself with these haunting melodies?
Or simply find companionship for my disdain?
Envious of movement, shy of trust, longing for togetherness.
God, don't let the song end now!

A flower wilts, I cannot save her.
My existence dims.
Skin tight pain is a flavor best colored in shades of blue and black.
Why is my pen so light when my eyes grow heavy?

What thought just performed on the stage of your mind?
Was it of me, and who I might be?
And is that thought wasted because I cannot answer?
How disjointed it feels to end with a question.
And yet, how normal.

The Whys Have It

If I do something to feel good,
then I am exploring the life I was given.
If I do something to feel better,
then I am using it as a way to cope.
In both cases, the actual act could be the same;
but one is filled with joy, while the other is corrupted by sorrow.
Thus, it is the reason behind the act,
not necessarily the act itself,
that should be questioned.

A Nice Way to Look at Failure

When I see my failures as life challenging me to improve,
then I am motivated to rise above those challenges.
When I see my failures as ugly parts of me,
then those failures sap my strength.
And I prefer to stand back up
rather than lay down and die.

The Right Tool

One cannot use Logic to give things meaning.
To do so would be like reducing your favorite song down to which notes were played.

One cannot use Emotion to make rational decisions.
To do so would mean that when you went shopping all you would buy is ice cream.

So You Even Fooled Yourself

In just three lines I told you no
Though you knew the words were coming
I never lied or gave you reason to doubt
But you held on to your precious hope

You left without a kiss goodbye
But you had hidden motives
You thought that I just couldn't see
In truth it was your game I wouldn't play

Then sing yourself a sweet sleep song
Drown-out the roar of reality
The longer you can stay asleep
The longer remain your dreams untainted

Your eyes teared when you spoke of it
Trembling lips in fear you hide
Needing honesty but you're not used to it
The words you spoke a complete surprise

Then sing yourself a sweet sleep song
Drown-out the roar of reality
The longer you can stay asleep
The longer remain your dreams untainted

Caring is too great a risk sometimes
But hiding ensures that love is denied
This vicious little circle surrounds you now
At least you say you tried
At least you say you tried

1:15 a.m.

I am defeated before the fight
there is no second-chance on the past
no reset button

And if I had the power but once
to cast a spell and return to the past
to change but one thing
I would have already wasted it

In truth, I weep less for what has been done
and more for the future I've already tainted
Because the possibilities of the future
are all I have left

I write songs of pain
because the hurt flows so freely
It's my joy I see slipping, too soon, away

Fragile Apathy

A fragile flask of emotion sits beside me.
As separate from me as I feel from the rest of humanity.

A satellite beams images of them through my walls
and onto the lonely electronic window I stare at.
For hours I watch them...
Jealous of the companionship they enjoy.
Add envy to my list of sins.

When I can't take it anymore,
I pick up my flask of feelings and carry it to my tiny porch.
The single yellow bulb of light makes a dull effort to chase away
the dark of night, but only succeeds in deepening my isolation.
A recording of my favorite sad song does the rest,
and my apathy can no longer be maintained...

My emotions burn as I empty the flask down my throat,
and the searing pain takes my breath away as I start to feel once more.
I bury my face in my hands
but they can't seal the leak that my eyes have sprung,
or muffle the banshee's wail that escapes my lips.
A scream that nobody hears.
An echo that reminds me why I keep this bottled up.

As I regurgitate my feelings back into their fragile flask,
quiet returns to the night air.
Only my puffy red eyes and the mucus dripping from my nose
belie that I had any feelings.
My stone-cold apathy is in control once more.
A necessary façade when you're all alone.

Musi©

Work speeds along,
almost as fast as my flying fingers stroking yet
another riff on my air guitar.
My head pulses, The energy burns,
Time Flies!
The Beat is the Drug, The Feedback the High.
The Feeling is a scar left, Not on your skin,
but in your head.

It changes you. It accompanies you.
It consoles you. It Excitcs you!
I am charged as long as the Bass thumps.
I am as strong as the shockwave that splits the Air.
As if the power supply that feeds the amp drives me
also.

And if the music stops, there remains only the
drab sound of Reality...
Returning me from my temporary Immortal state;
Tired
Bored
Human
That is, until the next track!

Living Deadly

The baleful symbols of
my heart, beg me a journey take.
Into it's depths I walk alone, not
sleeping, not awake.
And there a blasted
landscape still, before me stood
a lonely hill, the midnight moon awash with
gloom, with dread and tears my eyes did fill.
Upon the crest in silhouette, stood a lone and leafless
tree.
With hand-like branch in stark relief, it seemed to
beckon me.
In silence beckoned me.

I crossed the short but barren field and made the
dusty climb.
Beyond the crest a valley stretched, 'neath shadows
deep and wide.
Beneath the tree a ghoul did wait,
then t'wards me stepped with shambling gait,
with dead eyes saw and crooked claw
pointed to a path descending straight.
The moon was full, the air was still, my eyes were
wide with fright.

Because I knew this putrid corpse would be my guide this night.
He'd walk with me tonight.

We started down the rocky path that led into the vale.
And as we strode he pointed out, my bits of life revealed.
    All seemed gray or yellow-white,
    the colors bleached in fetid light,
    and broken dreams down crooked streams
    washed by and then were gone from sight.
We wandered through my lifetime past, those scattered bits of me.
I bowed my head and bit my lip, I couldn't bear to see.
It hurt too much to see.

Upon the ground a tattered book, 'twas one I used to read. It filled me full of wicked guilt, and painful aching need.
    Some hearts of steel and
    glass were spread
    along the ground they lay and bled.
    Some are gone and some bleed on,
    each drop on my behalf was shed.
There were some shiny pieces too, but they had dulled with time.

The whirlwind of my shattered life had coated them in grime.
There's simply too much grime.

My body was about faint, I ached to rest my head.
And so I leaned upon the ghoul, for strength, though he was dead.
   His rotting hand caressed my hair,
   there was no comfort he could share.
   In icy chill, 'neath lonely hill,
   for me I felt God had no care.
Uncertain if alive or dead for the loss which I had seen,
once more alone atop the hill, I sat beneath my tree.
My lonely dying tree.

Though it be dead it still must stand, to watch this forlorn place.
In silent pain this blasted land of sins I can't erase.
   My eyes too filled with tears to see
   a road that'd give escape to me.
   My love grown cold, my body old,
   heart rooted to this dying tree.
Then sitting here where I began, my journey's at its end.
If I live on I'll live alone, I'm dead to all my friends.
I've lost my every friend.

The Problem with Empathy

When a person suffers, they find it nearly impossible to empathize with another's sorrow.
This is because their own pain holds their attention with such force, that they can only focus on themselves.
But even when their pain is gone, they still have a hard time offering true empathy.
This is because when they feel good, it is difficult to remember how exquisitely awful their own suffering was.

So must it ever be:
Too wrapped up in your own pain
to much care about the pain of others.

Or
Incapable of comprehending the depth of another's plight, blinded by your own contentment.
It's a wonder that we even have a word that describes putting one's self in another's shoes, since it's so hard to do.

No Promises

My thoughts are unclear,
Evening bleeds into night.
Sleepless I lay in my bed.
Alone I try to calm my soul
with Rock & Roll
with strained words
with one more page in a book you've read.

My blood like a spell brings an oxygen rush
while your aura conflicts with my will.
Is it a mandate of God's?
Or a man's?
Or a child's?
That binds you from what you could feel.

On the thin edge of change
I nearly fell in.
And to whose regret will it be?
Unanswered questions need some attention:
Are you wanting?
Are you crying?
Are possibilities dying?
No time to unveil what I see.

My heart is not something I choose to unlatch.
I trust not when it sets itself free.
Your silence, my solace, a vengeance of sorts?
We can't make it?
We can't take it?
So again we break it, and I fear...
One wall too many, old wounds not quite healed,
Your touch, my caress – unpromised, unsealed.

An Unfortunate Epitaph

Fall's Chill.
The smell of dying trees losing their grip on consciousness,
finally succumbing to dormancy's power.
It is inevitable; their sleep finds them like a child too tired to play one more game of tag.
I walk past these trees in silence.
Accompanied only by a cool breeze,
the occasional die-hard runner,
and my thoughts.

I am searching.
I know you, though we may have never met.
I feel you, though we may have never touched.
I miss you.

Falling leaves, empty walkways,
fitting somehow my mood.
The roads stretch on,
winding their way past cities and mountains...
infinite in their paths.
I pause and wonder...
How many more walks must I take alone?

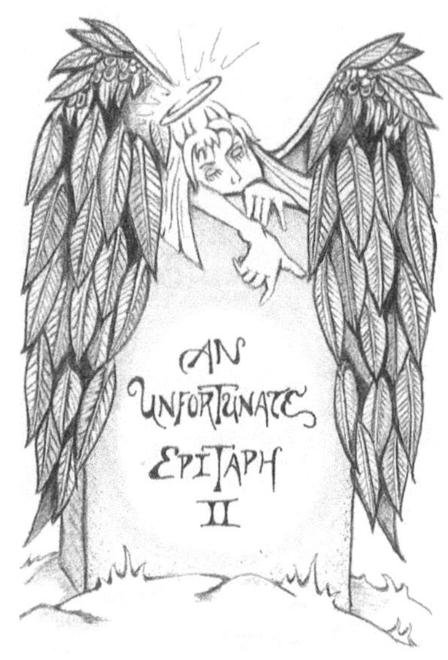

The sidewalk, autumn leaves,
falling down from sighing trees.
Walking, wondering if...
I'll ever find you,
ever know your name.

The icy wind's been with me far too long.
I know you're out there somewhere,
I can't be wrong.

Sleepy, dreams of you,
souls on fire, burning into you.
Lips they...
find your skin.
Starry eyes...
drink you in.

And when I wake alone I still feel you.
A ghost of lifetime's past, I ache for you.

Twilight, evening fades.
Moonbeams dying, I close the shades.
If I...
left this world today.
One sad epitaph
to etch on my grave... "He Never Found You"

One

Save me
Save me from my Demons
Save me

Save me
Save me from September
Save me from Waiting too Long
Save me

Save me
Save me from Fading
Save me from my Nature
Save me from today's Distraction
Save me

Save me
from my Fears, my Tears, my White Hair,
from my Longing, my Soliciting of Favors
and from my need to Sleep Late
Save me and I'll repay.

I too can save you
Together, Together, One.

Ordinary Corrosion

Sitting.
Staring at nothing in particular.
Sullen.
Out of character for someone who is happy.
Well, maybe not so strange as of late.
Its just that... Life's not the way I planned it.
In fact, as I think, all my plans were just vague fantasies,
and "real life" is what happened in-between my dreams.
I'm not sad.
I've got no specific reason to be sad.
Perhaps it's that I've realized how ordinary I am...
and I'd dreamed of so much more.
The spectacular life of my visions:
Adventure, Struggle, Triumph... Love.
So distant (except for the struggle part) from reality.
Will I wake every morning,
and live the same day over and over again?
Will I fall asleep every night,
reading a book about somebody else?
Like I said, I'm happy...
I'm ordinary.

Noise

The echoes off these concrete walls
reverberate in my skull
It's so loud
I'm constantly surrounded by raucous laughter
Empty calories
and meaningless activities
All necessary distractions to soothe hundreds of
angry minds
No one
Especially not those in the trap
Wants to face the bleak reality
-This is a life of useless repetition-
There are many things I could do
None that I want
It's too loud
Even things of true value
lose their luster behind walls
It's so draining

Annwyl

Fair maiden come and walk with me
to undying lands of green
Where music fills sweet air with sound
and beauty seldom seen;
by mortal eyes

There none speak of mine or thine
where eyes of black and cobalt shine
Where rosy cheeks for all do greet
and babbling brooks sing songs divine

Oh won't you come and walk awhile
past flower fern and glen
Leave this heart-sick world behind
forget the cares of men;
and deaths call

'Twixt mushroom ring there lies a key
the doorway to this place
Where sugared scents drip from skin
all blemish there erased

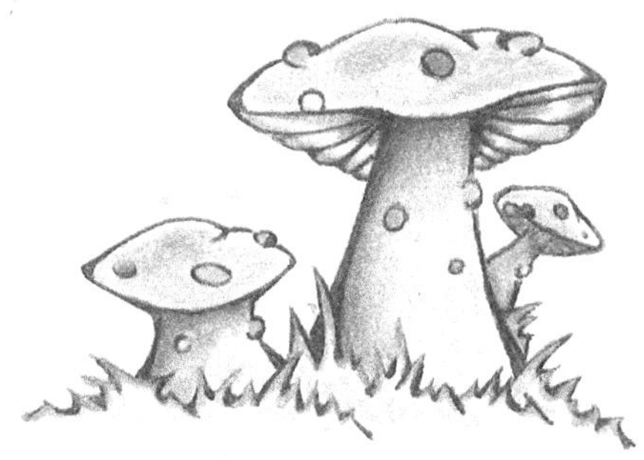

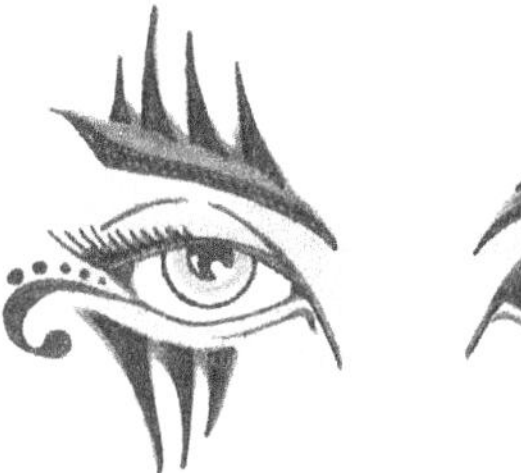

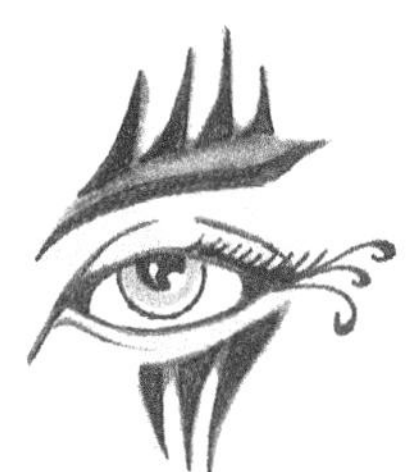

Let passion carry you away
and dance upon light feet
If you would but believe in this
Queen Nimue we might meet;
the way is open

Drink honeyed mead sip wine of gold
hold ancient treasures wealth untold
Unclouded eyes no Adam's sin
where free hearts float on gentle winds

In shadows cast by emerald hill
can one transform their shape at will
And love is made in hidden glade
where heady frothy passions spill;
drink deeply

So why not come and walk with me
down where the fair folk play
You'll 'ner again want for anything
let your sorrows fade away

The Smell of Black

Remember that smell?
You know, THAT one.
The one that hangs in the walls, the furniture, and the house of everyone's grandparents.
So distinct, yet almost unnoticeable because it's so familiar.
Cozy even.
How can it be?
So many different homes, so many different people
yet the smell is the same.
It must be the smell that's created by mixing all the odors of everything that ever had a scent over many, many years.
Kinda like crayons…

You know. You've done it.
You scribble a bunch of different colors together (which colors in which order being almost irrelevant).
Eventually you end up with some shade of Black.
Lighter or darker perhaps,
but nevertheless recognizable as black.
So, the next time your nose comes across that smell,
think for a moment…
Is this not truly the smell of Black?!?

Why Pleasure is so Short

Pleasure is but a moment's rest between Pains
Were it to last any longer, I would become too attached
And then I could never survive the drop from the High to the Lows
Pain is just a catalyst for change
And by the sheer length of time I find myself in pain
I deduce that a sadistic divine something-or-other thinks I need to change
A LOT

Too Many Voices

Where a scream is barely noticed
A whisper has no hope
With so many voices yelling
One alone can't cope
If we all continue screaming
In hopes our voice is heard
What use is conversation
When the roar obscures the words

How not to stay employed after your paper airplane takes a wrong turn:

"Well I may be a 30 year old adolescent, but BOSS spelled backwards makes you a double S.O.B."
It was probably for the best. That Dick was never going to have a sense of humor

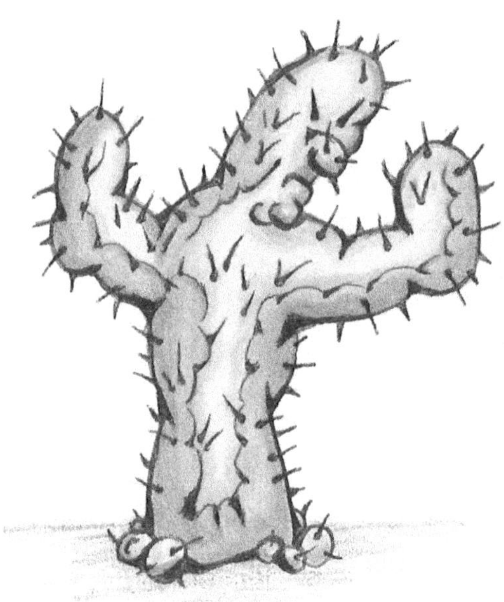

A Cactus
doesn't get
Hugs

The Death of a Romantic

Sweet and awful in the same breath
The sweet I crave and awful is my death
Though I die it once or one thousand times
in the end love will kill with its sultry designs

You cry when you're touched by the silver screen
But when it's yours to possess in reality
no affection, rejection, roll your eyes in mockery
You fear being intimate when it's not on TV

You laughed when I tried to romance you, enhance you
And you turned away when I tried to dance with you
Then I hear your kind when you speak your mind
how you wish for one sensitive man left to find
Now I'll tell you plainly, though you will never listen
If you keep on laugh'n then you can keep on wish'n
For no body's too fine nor face clouds my mind
when I open my heart you can't jeer at my rhyme

So unearth the darkness in men if you must
But we can't truly love those unworthy of trust
My face carved from stone leaves you feeling alone
Then I'll send you on your way, and I'll go my own

What is Truly Dangerous

I wanted to feast on life,
to drink deeply from its bottomless cup.
To dive into the inscrutable depths of emotion.
But I had to be careful, the world is a dangerous place.

I wanted to run with the pack,
until I was gasping for air.
My chest heaving until my heart burst with exhilaration.
But I had to be careful, the world is a dangerous place.

I wanted to explore every peak,
wander strange mountains,
until I got so lost that I'd long for home.
But I had to be careful, the world is a dangerous place.

I wanted to feel silky forbidden passion.
Run my hands over every inch of her skin,
until I passed out from the ecstasy.
But I had to be careful, the world is a dangerous place.

I wanted to start a fight I couldn't win.
I wanted to touch the flame just to experience the burn.
I wanted to choose the uncertain path that called me.
But I had to be careful, the world is a dangerous place.

What I found was that,
with or without my carefulness,
the world will always be a dangerous place.
But avoiding what I truly wanted out of fear…
That has been fatal.

Guilt, Guilt, Guilt = Guilty

This word it defines me
Its attractions denied me
All that was good in this life.
I let it control me
Rob and expose me
Machine-gunned with bullets of strife.
Now I bear it inside me
At it's whim it derides me
Even when I have nothing to fear.
Its pain still shoots through me
It so easily moves me
What would I be without it so near?

Becoming Joyful

Reason can be burdensome.
But so can being bereft of it.
For my own sanity I must liberate myself from being too serious, prudent, scientific, etc…
While still shunning blindness, foolishness, and irrationality.

I can be Carefree
Because I'm Insightful.
I can be Joyful
In spite of having learned the hard way.
I can be OK with paradoxes
Not because they are acceptable
But because - such is life –
(And no amount of my bitching will change that they exist).

Some things I must Accept
Not because I've Given Up
But because I've found that there are things I can't Change
(And I can live with that).
Wisdom, not smarts, is what breeds Joy.

Untitled:

I AM RESILIENT
BUT NOT EASEFULLY
I WORK TOO HARD AT IT
WHEN I'D PREFER JUST TO BE

Oh Say What is Truth

I would certainly like to know what truly “IS”.
But I find myself so poorly equipped for this task that I doubt it is within my reach.
So many people in this world claim to “know” the truth.
However, so far, I’ve found them all to be full of shit.
Their senses lie to them just as surely as mine do to me.
So how do they dare look at me with such certainty?
Only through the force of their conviction,
-their faith-
do they get me to listen with any serious interest.
Because their “proof” is weak at best.
When I get caught up in the whirlwind of their claims,
their passion has an attraction that pulls me into their narrative.
The “storm” in them stirs up a storm in me.
But then I realize…
Attraction to passion is probably the worst possible reason to align one’s self.
Eventually their façade cracks.
Eventually it is revealed that - for all their bluster –
they are just as blind, deaf, and dumb as I am.
Their so called “truth” may have some value…
But it is far from being absolute.
While I’d bet that Absolute Truth exists;
I wouldn’t bet on our tiny brains being capable of comprehending it.

A Precarious Balance

Rules and freedom work well together, so long as the one does not overburden the other.

It seems a line so subtle, that only the most vigilant will notice when the balance has been tipped. And if we wait too long before setting the balance aright, then eventually imbalance becomes codified as the new normal.

Thus, even if we are laboring beneath the weight of a preponderance of rules, we can be incited to bear that weight in the name of Justice.

But Law is not Justice.

When there is a balance between Law and Freedom, then the rules are a shield; protecting freedom from anarchy.

But when we make too many rules; they become a sword - separating us from freedom by condemning us to punishments which have (too often) been far from Just, and against which mankind stands completely naked.

When we conflate Rules with Justice, we settle for fairness, abandon the search for truth, and excuse the alienation of inalienable rights.

When we conflate Law with Good, we elevate our man made rules above the laws of nature, and grind up the men and women whose nature offends our arrogance with the machine of our own making.

Freedom needs space. It is messy. It spills out of the nice mcasured boxes we would keep it in.

So, for as much as we might wish otherwise, the gift of Freedom is best protected by the absence of our small minded interference.

However, because people are too intolerant or too wild to respect such a gift; rules will always be on the verge of strangling it.

Your epic success

If you wanted me to be afraid
Then you succeeded
If you wanted me to feel immense sorrow
Then you succeeded
My hands still shake in your presence, anticipating the next kick
Everyday I look at my child's picture and my heart breaks anew

If you wanted me to lose hope
Then you succeeded
If you wanted me to feel alone and weak
Then you succeeded
Both my mind and body ache as I work to keep my humanity
Even if you let me go, who would ever treat me normally?

If you wanted to destroy my future,
Then you succeeded
If you wanted to pull every tear from my eyes
Then you succeeded
I will grow old (inside or out) unable to care for myself
I have nothing left but a cold lump in my throat

Though your punishment was an epic success, you will never be done with me
All the pain I've described (and more) has done nothing to stir your compassion
How much revenge is enough?
Was not my own lack of compassion, my own act of revenge, the basis on which you claimed the right to punish me?

Suicide Watch

Tic Toc goes the clock
My spinning head just won't stop spinning.
Wait, did I say that already?
    Tic Toc
Cold hands, no god-damn socks. Yes, I am Tic talking with myself.
I am naked, I got no bed
I lay on a tray instead   Humor helps.
    Tic Toc
It's for my own good - Tic Toc.
Stop looking in on me, I need to jack off - Tic Toc.
Stop slamming doors, I need to sleep - Tic Toc.
Stop talking about me like I'm not right in front of you!
    Tic Toc
Hours take days to get through – Tic Toc.
Now I want to kill both myself and them too – Tic Toc.
For the first time in my life it makes sense to fling my poo – Tic Toc.
I'd use a shoe as a pillow, but I ain't got no shoes.
Wait, did I say that already?

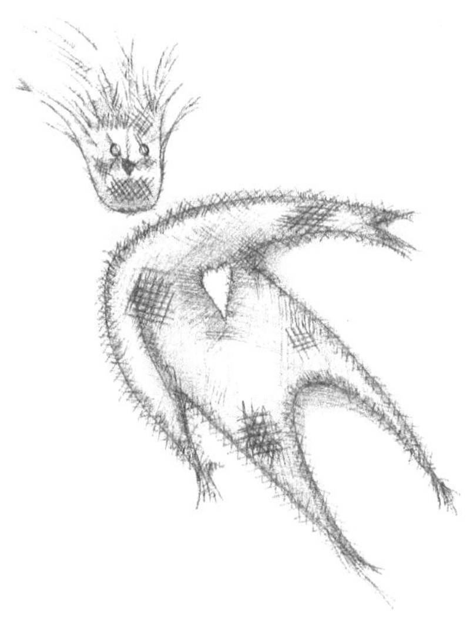

The Jesus Freaks Song

(in the key of D)

V.1- Well he sees you in the spring time,
and he sees you in the fall.
He sees you when you're all dressed up,
and when you've nothin' on at all.
He sees you when you're doing right,
and when you're doing wrong…
So you'd better not touch yourself
when you're sitting on the john.

Ch.1- Cuz it's Jesus in your morning song
it's prayers to Jesus all night long,
it's Jesus who will make things go your way.
It's Jesus who's been keepin' lists
of church attendance and when you're pissed.
Jesus Freaks are quick to tell you what you can't say.

V.2- Well He counts the times He sees you sin,
and when you fail to pray.
He counts the hairs upon your head,
and the tithing you should pay.
Now I'm not sure when He looks down,
what He hopes to see…
But I'm fairly sure He's tired of watch'n
your hypocrisy.

Ch.2- Still it's Jesus in your morning song,
it's prayers to Jesus all day long,
it's Jesus who will make things go your way.
It's Jesus who's been keep'n lists
of church attendance and when you're pissed.
I'm sorry folks, Jesus Freaks are here to stay.

V.3- Now, there's prob'ly some who think I'm crass,
and some who want to kick my ass
for making fun of Jesus Freaks this way.
But remember when you hear me speak,
that Jesus turned the other cheek.
So if you serve Him you'll forgive me for what I say -
right away.

The only prayer I still offer in Jesus's name:
"Please save me from Your followers."

It's funny how much they ask You to forgive them;
and then make rules that are so unforgiving.

It's funny how closely they listen to Your words about You saving them;
and how deaf when You ask them for their help saving others.

I marvel at all the wonders of art and architecture built by Christianity;
and then wonder: How much of it is necessary to love one's neighbor?

What kind of mansion do You keep great Master,
when only the threat of punishment,
or the promise of reward,
keeps your disciples in line with Your word?

The Fools Journal: Entry F – 1: The Dilemma of The Suit of Wands (Fire)

Too much passion,
and energy scatters in
too many directions.
Overly wild; unable to create
an abundance of success.

Too much discipline,
and passion wilts.
And thus are many great
ideas extinguished by
unimaginative people.

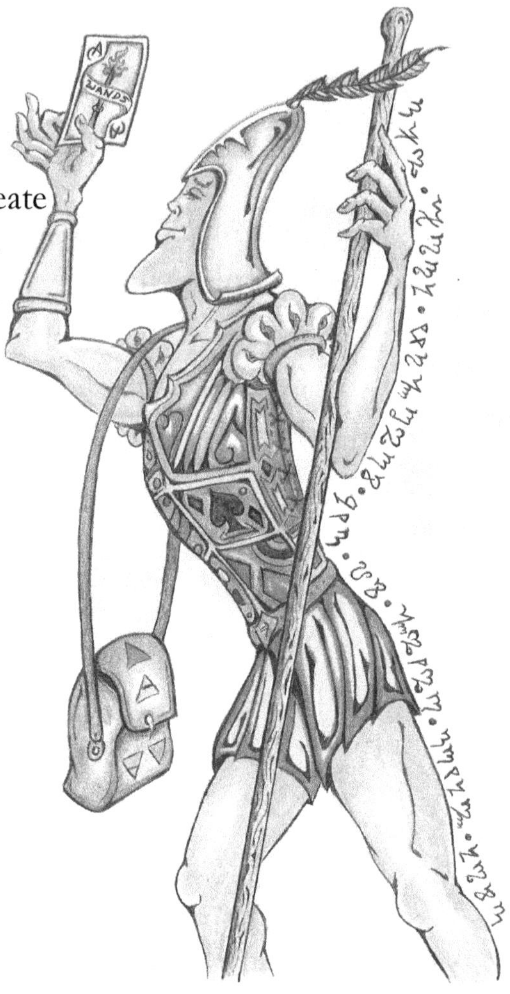

untitled

I am the gentle curves of Love
I am the harsh edges of Wild Passion
I am the Light
and I am the Darkness
Am I just learning this?
Or just remembering things forgotten?

Is there any love left for me?

Love, pull me into you.
Breathe deeply,
let me fill you.
I miss the taste of new sweat on clean skin
and the sugar of your lips.
I miss the marks of your nails down my back
and the flicker of candlelight in your eyes.
Our flesh burns like paper.
Are we even real?
What's left after this moment ends?
Will I ever feel your heat again?

What about what I wanted

I've always been a dreamer
But that's not what the world wanted for me
They were steel and I was glass
They decided that I'd make a good doorknob
A means to someone else's ends
Useless except when being used
How do I change these stars?
I want to be a father to my child
I want to see the world
I want to create something spectacular
Before I drift away
Before I fade

Choice?

The only roads are the ones you take
It seems like it's your choice to make
Like the pie-in-the-sky is for you to bake
– But your choices are so few

While more than whim of fate or chance
There's so much weight to circumstance
Born in a skirt or wearing pants
– There's so much you didn't choose

An Apology

I'm sorry I was sleeping
There's so much I didn't know
I used to have secrets worth keeping
That's why you woke up on your own

A Matter of Faith

I believe that mortal death is but a doorway.
A doorway to more life.
As I ponder this belief, it leads me to other conclusions:
If more life comes next,
then a fear of death is actually a fear of living.
Since to fear living results in a failure to truly live…
then fear, not dying, is the only true death.

To My Darling Dew Drop

Reality could never compare
to your unrequited ghost.
Thirty years now past
and I still dream about you.
How can what-might-have-been be so sticky?

untitled

If you live your life striving for the vision you chose for yourself,
then there is nothing to rebel against.

Disposable People

There have always been disposable people.
The proverbial lepers of every age.
I was just shocked to find that I was one of them.
"Not me" I cry out to whomever might listen. "I have value!"
But just because I know in my heart that it's true,
doesn't mean anyone else must acknowledge it.

I was once like those who mattered; like you.
I couldn't have cared less that my disabled neighbor was also a great singer.
I couldn't have cared less that the destitute brown woman was also a good mother.
I couldn't have cared less that some inmate was battling a hopeless situation, yet was still working to reform himself.
I couldn't have cared less that a starving child in Africa might be another Einstein.
I couldn't have cared less that a struggling student in some ghetto was trying to fight past the noise and fear to make her dream of a better life come true.
I was unmoved by their struggles, and they were the ones trying.
I was immune to their cries, like the butcher is to his soon-to-be meat.
Because they were disposable.

And then I too was discarded… so,
I know why you don't answer my letters.
I understand why my pleas for relief are ignored.
I'm not surprised that my efforts don't impress you.
And why, when I'm not invisible, I am at best an inconvenience.

But knowing why you are this way doesn't make it sting less.
So I scream from the depths of my soul: "I am not disposable!"
But, like the only man with ears on the planet of the deaf,
no one notices.

Another leprosy-free group of you heedlessly shuffles past the heap of human trash,
on your way to something that matters.
And I don't waste my breath, 'cuz I know I'm just one of those disposable.

All That I've Lost

My daddy once told me: "Son, be careful what you do."
"No matter what you build in life, they'll try and take it away from you."
Well I really didn't listen, and married me a wife.
But now the girl has left me, and I'll owe her all my life.
    - She took it all-
Well, I drove down to Vegas, in a brand new Cadillac.
Lady Luck was with me, until I bet it all on black.
To win back my money, they let me bet my car…
When you're walk'n in the desert, the road home seems oh so far.
    - I lost it all-
You see, I wound up with so little, thought I'd noth'n left to lose.
Working my fingers down, but I still can't buy new shoes.
It all made me feel so angry, that I went and broke the law…
Now they've locked me up with no parole, so they truly have it all.
    - I finally lost it all-

Anxiety Attack

My labored breath comes in gasps.
Some invisible hand strangles each one.
How can it be so hard to draw air when nothing's blocking it?
I gulp down more panic with each sweaty second!
    -drowning in a sea of oxygen.

I want to pound my head against the wall.
Maybe I can knock myself into blissful unconsciousness.
My body drops into survival mode.
But there's no one to fight and nowhere to flight.
    -everything's closing in!

Breathe deep and slow they tell me;
    -there are no answers.
Try meditation they tell me;
    -nothing helps.
This shouldn't happen to a strong person;
    -I'm not in control.
    -I can't stop it.
    -I'm weak!

Will someone please tell the evil clown who's twisting my guts
that my stomach isn't one of his balloon animals!
    -Then I puke.
I warned you I wasn't in control.
    -sorry about your shoes.

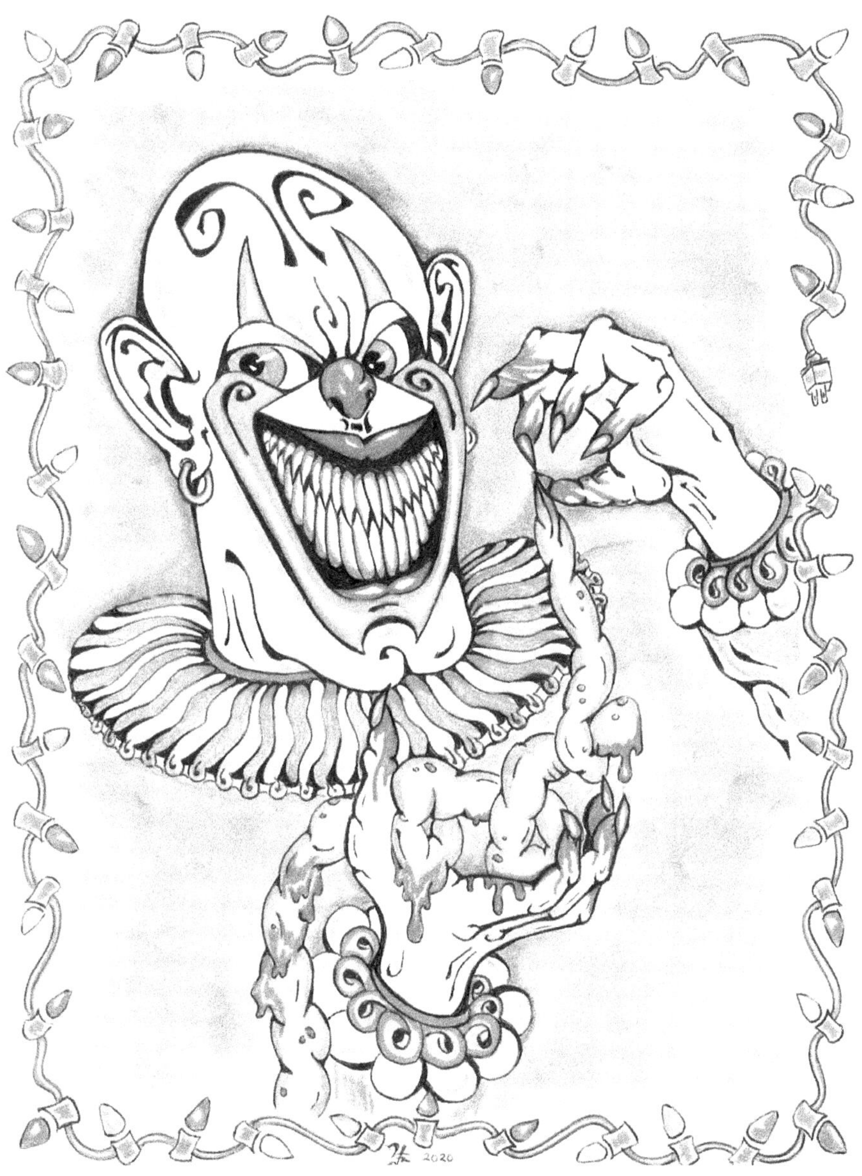

Head Monkeys
(in the key of A)

V.1- How do I think through the things that I'm feeling
How do I write the perfect words to a song
How do I live in this world without drinking
How do I right the ones I've wronged

Br.1- Why do I wonder if my path is the best
And why do I care if I'm passing your tests
If life is a race then I think I should rest
But that's not the way it's 'gonna be

Ch.1- I'm not living: Existing doesn't mean that I'm alive
I'm not living; when the best I can do is just survive
I'm not living; if the hope that was inside of me is dead
I'm not living; when I wrestle with the monkeys in my head

V.2- Why do I need my life to be sweeter
How do I know what it is I should be
Why do I search for a love that is deeper
Before I know what's really me

Br.2- What can I do to get you out of my head
Leave me alone, did you hear what I said
If you won't go away then I'm better off dead
The monkeys are swinging again

Ch.2- I'm not living; with these questions turning circles in my mind
I'm not living; if I let go of the answers that I find
I'm not living; when I spend the day asleep within my bed
I'm not living; when I wrestle with the monkeys in my head

Br.3- Do you know what you're doing? Then you'd better not try
Close up your mouth boy or you're 'gonna catch flies
Don't step 'outta line and don't open your eyes
The monkeys are swinging again

Ch.3- I'm not living: Because I'm breathing doesn't mean that I'm alive
I'm not living; when I dream about the ways I 'wanna die
I'm not living: You couldn't ever hear me when I said…
I'm not living; when I wrestle with the monkeys in my head
when I wrestle with the monkeys in my head

The Temple of the Moon

Daily my heart leaps anticipating your arrival.
Tiny Goddess of both seen and hidden charms.
I came to your temple bending freely.
And before your improbable altar,
I become a child.

Your perfect sacred circle glowing.
The arch of backs and necks in similitude.
Skin kissed by sun and shadow both.
And I imagine your taste.

Unknowingly you give your gift,
refined edges define every curve,
leading to only imagined depths,
yet enough to extract the fire in which I burn.

How I ache for more than this glimpse,
to see beyond your veil.
Ever were my stars a guide to this weightless burden.
Too coincidental to be explained by choice or chance.

But far too late did my head find my heart.
Now tortuous longing accompanies each deep breath.
Both of us held, yet untouched.
And so I beg my ecstatic doom,
please change my fate.

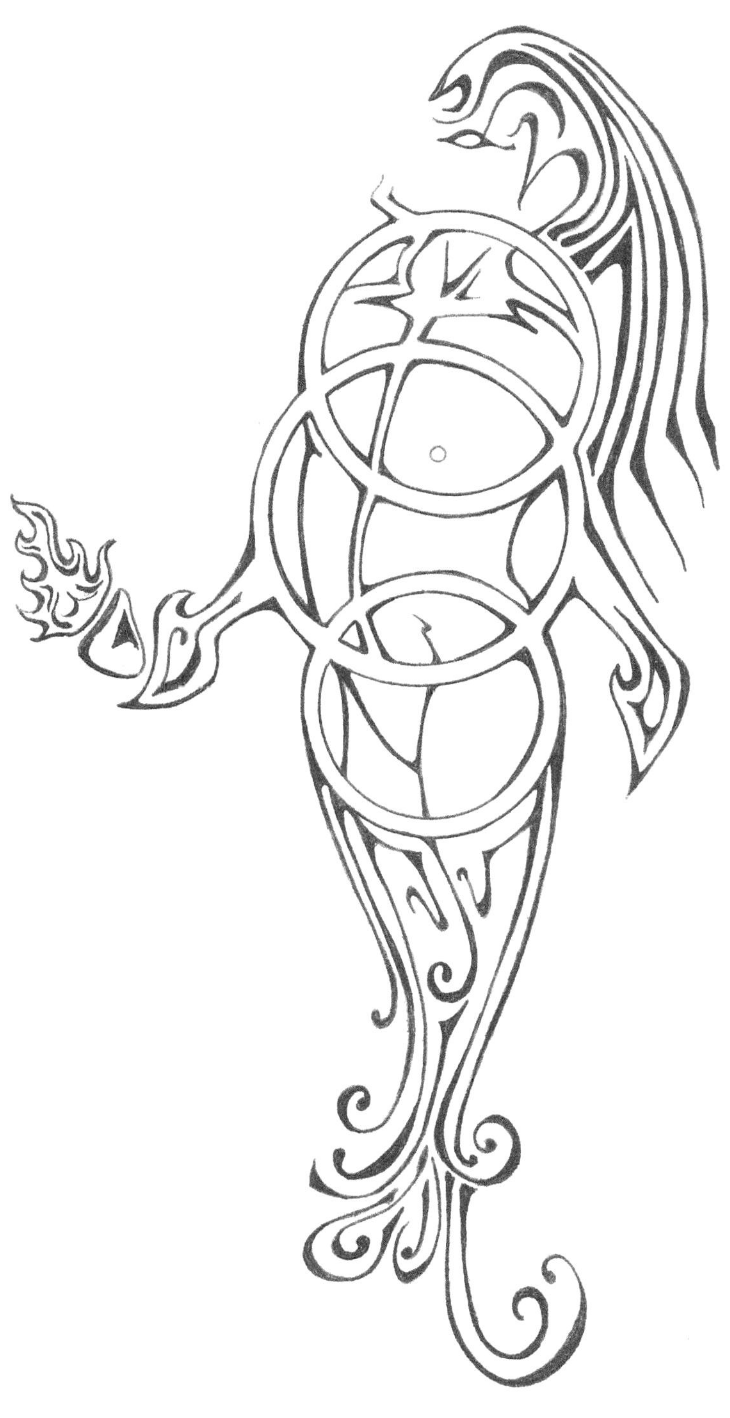

Last Goodbye
(in the key of D)

V.1- I know, that you'll go.
I tried to tell you how I hurt,
but you don't care. No, you don't care.

V.2- I say, will you stay?
I need some time for you to see me,
but you're not there. No, you're not there.

Ch.1- When I first saw you, I adored you.
And when I kissed you, I felt that sparks flew.
And if you loved me then I would love you too.
I would love you too.
When I touched you, I thought that I knew.
And so I asked you, you said yes, I do.
We came together and didn't have a clue, of
things that we'd go through.

V.3- Eyes of frost, have icy costs.
I am broken and you are frozen,
there's no more need to lie. Those tears don't
mean you cried.

V.4- Lost needs, and dark seeds.
They grew between us and strangled me.
So here's my last goodbye. Here's my last
goodbye.

Ch.2- You're silky skin and heart of stone,
they left their marks on my own.
Where did the time go? I think what might have
been. I think what might have been.
I look in your eyes and I realize,
your heart has wandered and mine has died.
I've gone beyond why, so here's my last
goodbye; here's my last goodbye;
herc's my last goodbye

What can my child believe in?
(in the key of G)

V.1- I heard the man on the radio,
said all the people were feeling low.
It seems that things didn't really go the way they all planned.
I've seen their faces out on the street,
so many gazes I couldn't meet.
They're barely standing on their feet as I walk away…
and I walk away.

Ch.1- What can my child believe in? What's left for him?
What's left for me?
Show me somethin' worth believ'n
or I can't see a reason to want to stay.

V.2- We sold those things that once made us strong.
We gave our rights away for leaders' wrongs.
Greed and hate can silence freedom's song - It's been done before.
There's no new lands left for us to find,
if Tyranny's here it can't be left behind.
If we don't take back our rights in time, well then we're stuck here.

Ch.1 What can my child believe in? What's left for him?
What's left for me?
Show me somethin' worth believ'n
or I can't see a reason to want to stay.

V.3- I held your hand and you held mine.
Four short years, it seemed we'd do just fine.
I guess it always seems we'll have more time - until it's gone.
My life feels cold since I went away.
I gave the sun up for a cloudy day.
It's so hard to see you through the haze, how do I find you?

Ch.1- What can my child believe in? What's left for him?
What's left for me?
Show me somethin' worth believ'n
or I can't see a reason to want to stay.

Outro: What can my child believe in? (x3)

Shane`s Storm - A Suicide by Overdose Story

You took an early train. Another day of rain.
You're feeling less than sane, and can't see past the pain.
    What you running from?
    What you running from now?
    Things will follow you – You'll find out how.
You say it's over. The storm is blowing out.
If it was over, you could have come back down.

Another demon day. Your thoughts are on display.
Too many things to say. You start to lose your way.
    What you headed for?
    What you headed for now?
    You can't carry this – So lay it down.
You said it's over. The storm had fizzled out.
If it was over, you should have come back down.

You slip into the night. You're running from the light.
So tired of the fight, that you forget what's right.
Sliding down again.
Can't come home again now.
Flying high again – Can't come back down.
Now it's over. We know it's over now.
This end is final. The storm has burned you out.

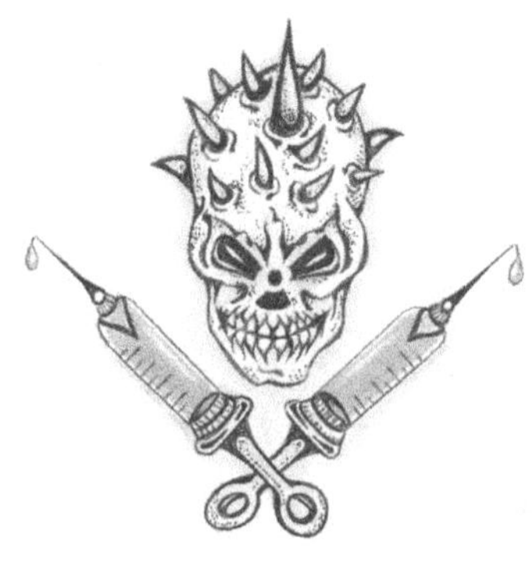

Hold On

I must hold on.
I must hold on.
You want me to believe in things I've never seen.
You want me to concede to live inside your dream.
Why should I grow old in a life I find so cold?
How are you so bold that you force me into your mold?
I must hold on.
I must hold on.
I slide along her skin,
I breathe her in, she holds my face.
Where you see only sin,
I found heaven and God's grace.
While your righteous fight goes on, it's your hollow life that's gone.
Who are you to say I'm wrong? It's my body and it's my song.
I must hold on.
I must hold on.
Our flesh will turn to dust, when time it sets us free.
You live in fear of Hell, but those chains they don't hold me.
How do you hold on with a hope that's so far gone?
It's with glee you preach I'm wrong, but I'm happy with my song.
I'm happy I held on.

Time

Born in flesh I
feel my heart beat
Young blood flows strong
but then it slips away

The rhythm of life keeps time
But it steals my heart

I wake up dying
though my pulse still thrums
The rhythm drives on
but there's no cheating time

The hands of clocks spin on
And all I have is now

Born from stars I
feel my fate's tide
Another day gone
How soon will I fade

Every day there's pain
And there's no one to blame

Born in flesh I
feel my heart beat
Blood still flows strong
but Time must run away

Humor for Dad

Dear Dad,
Since you're depressed about losing your leg to diabetes, I thought of some amputation jokes in hopes of cheering you up:

- If you were a Lord of the Rings character who would you be?
  - Leg-o-less
- If you were Native American where would you live?
  - In an ampu-tee-pee
- Why wouldn't I want you as my attorney?
  - Our case wouldn't have a leg to stand on
- Why won't they let you drive anymore?
  - You'd just cut people off
- What's your new favorite firearm?
  - A sawed-off shotgun
- Why are you no good at riddles?
  - Because now you're always stumped
- Why can't you be a sailor?
  - You're afraid of choppy water (Yeah, yeah - they can't all be gold)

Now, if you're still depressed, just think of all the benefits there are to being an amputee: You can't stub your toe, you can't sprain your ankle, and you no longer have athletes foot. But apparently you can still put your foot in your mouth (at least according to mom), so watch out for that.
Dad, I hoped this helped cheer you up. But if not, I ain't too worried about this pissing you off. Because without a leg, you certainly can't kick my ass!
- Keep your chin up –
You're on the last leg of this mortal journey.
Love

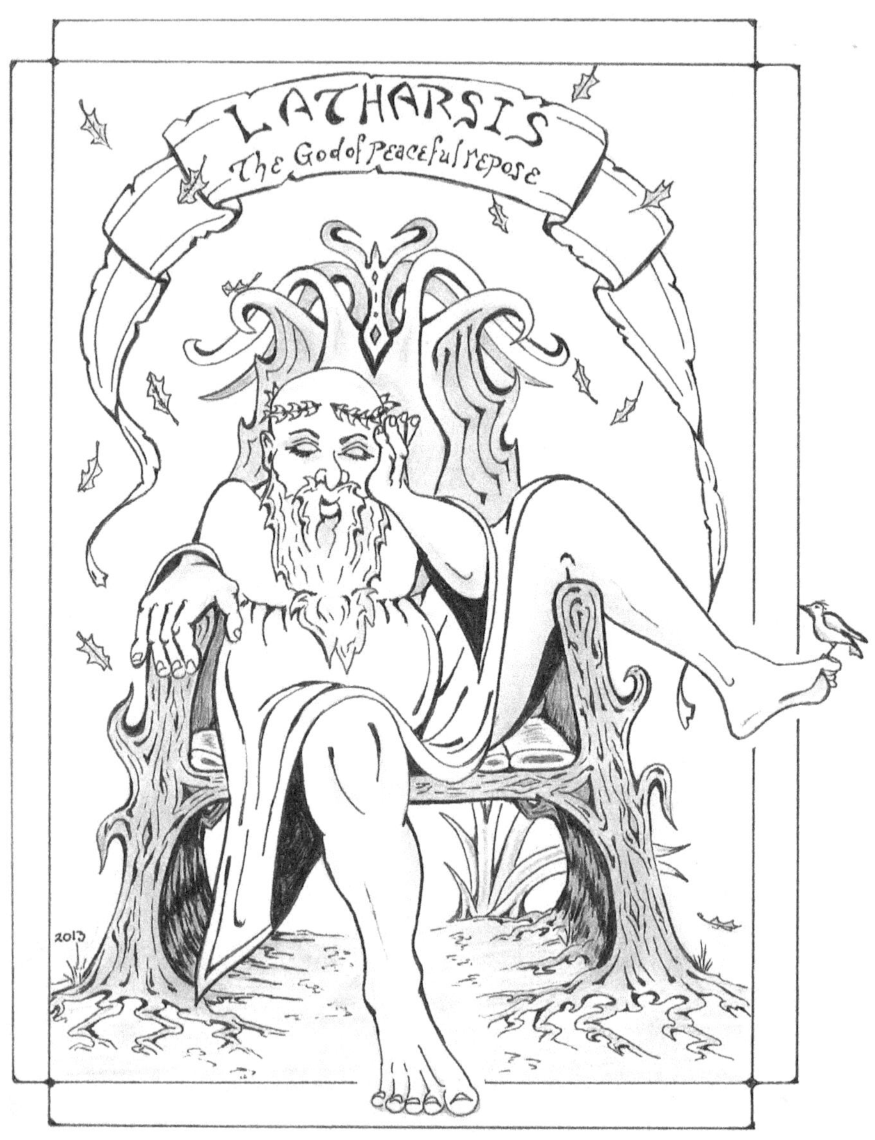
LATHARSIS
The God of Peaceful Repose
2013

The Blessed God of Sleep

Another day of burdens
a lump within my chest
My efforts all ring hollow
and my body begs for rest
The weights that I must carry
the woes that I have seen
Makes Earth a place so dreary
that I look forward to my dreams
The God of sleep he finds me
as I lay down on my bed
I welcome his embrace so he can soothe my aching head

The night is full of wonder
there's a castle full of gold
At my command the thunder
and my hands shoot lightning bolts
My feet break from the ground
no wings yet still I fly
The winds the only sound as
I pass the eagles by
The God of sleep he knows me
He is generous with His Gift
His magic heals my mind so I'm not jumping off of cliffs

The waking world's derision
has been a curse for me
The world of dreams a harbor
a beloved reality

Romans 9: 20-21

I am not God's Picasso
I am not God's silver cup
I am one of many vessels with the dubious title
"made unto dishonor"
But can the pot say to the Potter:
"Why did you make me thus?"
And why would the Potter hear the pot's complaint?
Were the pot remade into a priceless vase
it would leave the Potter without a pot to piss in

So who am I, so bold, so audacious, to complain?
At least I wasn't made for pissing
I'm more like a mop bucket…
Always invited to the party, but not with a place at the table
I'm invited only so afterwards, I can pick up the fallen bits of fun
that those "made unto honor" got to enjoy

I'm told I should be grateful
but for what I'm not quite sure
For even if I were encrusted with jewels
or gilt with the finest gold
I would still only merit a place in the closet

No, I am not God's silver cup
And knowing this wounds my soul
A broken spirit
It's not terminal, but it's probably permanent
Not that anyone cares what the mop bucket thinks

The Myth of Sisyphus, meets Jack & Jill, meets My Life

Jack's plea deal, roll this stone up a hill
It will take a lot of effort
Then we'll kick it back down
Off the hill you must bound
And you'll repeat this for ever after

'Round the ten-thousandth time, Jack resents the steep climb
is there any real point to me trying?
Well didn't you know
That's how punishment goes
It's forever and in this we're not lying

But surely there'd be some good lesson for me
Some value to all of this work
No, what we want is control
and a fun puppet show
You're a patsy at whom we can smirk

Now the hell of the hill is finally revealed
All this effort that never builds comfort
In this fire I still burn
And there's nowhere to turn
It's their game and I cannot escape it

Why Enlightenment is so Elusive (Don't read it - spit it!)

Discovering some new understanding, some bit of new truth is always a dangerous prospect, why? Because biting into the apple of knowledge threatens all our pretty little lies. Carefully constructed yet unconscious, these self-built sticky coping strategies abound, made to shield our delicate minds from a world full of discomfort and doubt.

Those illusions, those necessary self deceptions flee before the light of superior perception; but quickly regroup in the darkness of our psyche and, with the strength of old habits, the security of a well-worn path demand, that we ignore the call to be enlightened.

We'd all like to think of ourselves as the kind who, upon discovering new light would be brave and abandoned the inferior paths of our minds, and immediately change our ways. But that's just another of those pretty little stories we tell - the ones that keeps all of our cowardly acts hidden at the bottom of a deep mental well.

Thus, in the name of comfort, wrapped in a warm blanket of illusions (both seen and unknown) we find reasons to ignore the gift that the apple tried to bestow. And in spite of the light's attempt to expose our delusions we close the shutters on its rays of disruption, too invested in our shadowy maze to endure the pain of its deconstruction.

Despite the new understanding provided by the light, despite the glorious knock-down power of new truth's might, we cling to the illusions we built into mansions, so our lies can keep us thinking highly of our pathetic selves, and excuse our rampant dysfunctions.

<u>The Fool's Journal</u>: Doorway 13 – DEATH

It's been so long since I cried actual tears that I forgot how cold they feel as they run down my cheek. But the stoicism imposed upon me by my harsh environment could not stem their flow at the news of your passing.

You exited this life without ever seeing me achieve stability. And while that was probably an inevitability, it means you were the only solid foundation that I ever had. Now I don't know how to face the rest of my life in a world without your comforting presence - without the unconditional safe harbor you provided.

There was this tender part of me that used to daydream about our imagined reunion: Oh the joy of falling into your waiting arms, and the flood of happy emotions as we embraced for the first time in over a decade!

But now that hope, that single ray of sunshine, is as cold and dead as your corpse. And I must bury that broken dream just as deeply if I want to survive the weight of my remaining years. For the loss of this hope is too painful to ever exhume again.

As I sit here trying to mop up this puddle of emotions that I'd rather not feel, the daily circus of curses and irrationalities impose themselves upon my fragile mind… Heedless of how much more offensive they are in this moment than they were yesterday; unconcerned that I hate them more right now than I normally do; indifferent to the pain in my heart that must be similar to the one that killed you.

How do I say a proper goodbye in this place? How do I grieve with the ugly, useless churning of rancid walking meat-puppets who are constantly brushing up against my

emotional wounds?
Today more than ever, I don't want to be here. But I must endure it anyway. And the lack of even the slightest respite makes me wish that I could join you in death.
I have so many regrets. But regardless of how broken a road I was traveling, I always knew I had a place to call my home. Now that's no longer true, I find it so much harder to feel safe, and so much harder to say goodbye.

I was born a Magical Being, but...

All the mystical essence of life was sucked from my heart when I accepted the labels that others clothed me with.
Every wonderful and wonder-filled experience was stained by the dark weight of believing I was sinful.
And what can a child so burdened ever hope to become but the sinner he was told he was?

I've cried my tears for my dispelled innocence; no amount of wishing can revive the magic once stolen.
All I have left is today, and maybe tomorrow's potential. So I refuse to reduce the glorious magnitude of my remaining journey down to a never-satisfied list of religious "*Do's and Don'ts*".
That is not spirituality.
No glory awaits those who grab hold of self-indentured servitude.

KILL THE MONSTER

You love your pitchforks and torches.
The glint of passionate fire reflecting off sharp edges was meant to fill me with fear.
Your metaphorical steel rips into my very real, and very tender flesh.
Every century has its monsters to kill.

But have you ever considered the possibility that you're angry chanting and your torch-lit dancing we're why I bared my fangs?
Have you ever stopped to think that, being terrified of your boot, might be why the dog bites?

The mob always believes they are making things better.
The energy of the crowd is both the stimulant to scream "*Burn the Witch!*" as well as the anonymity to hide its participants from the guilt of looking at their ash-covered hands after the flames die down.

If my pain pleases you, how dare you think you are better than me?
Only hypocrites believe they can beat the good into another's soul.
My sickness it seems, is the only one worthy of punishment.
How yours got on the excused list, I will never know.

In a hundred years, what will your progeny say?
Do you think they will be proud of your mob's violence?
Or will they shake their collective heads in disbelief and shame; wondering how you could possibly justify so much hate?

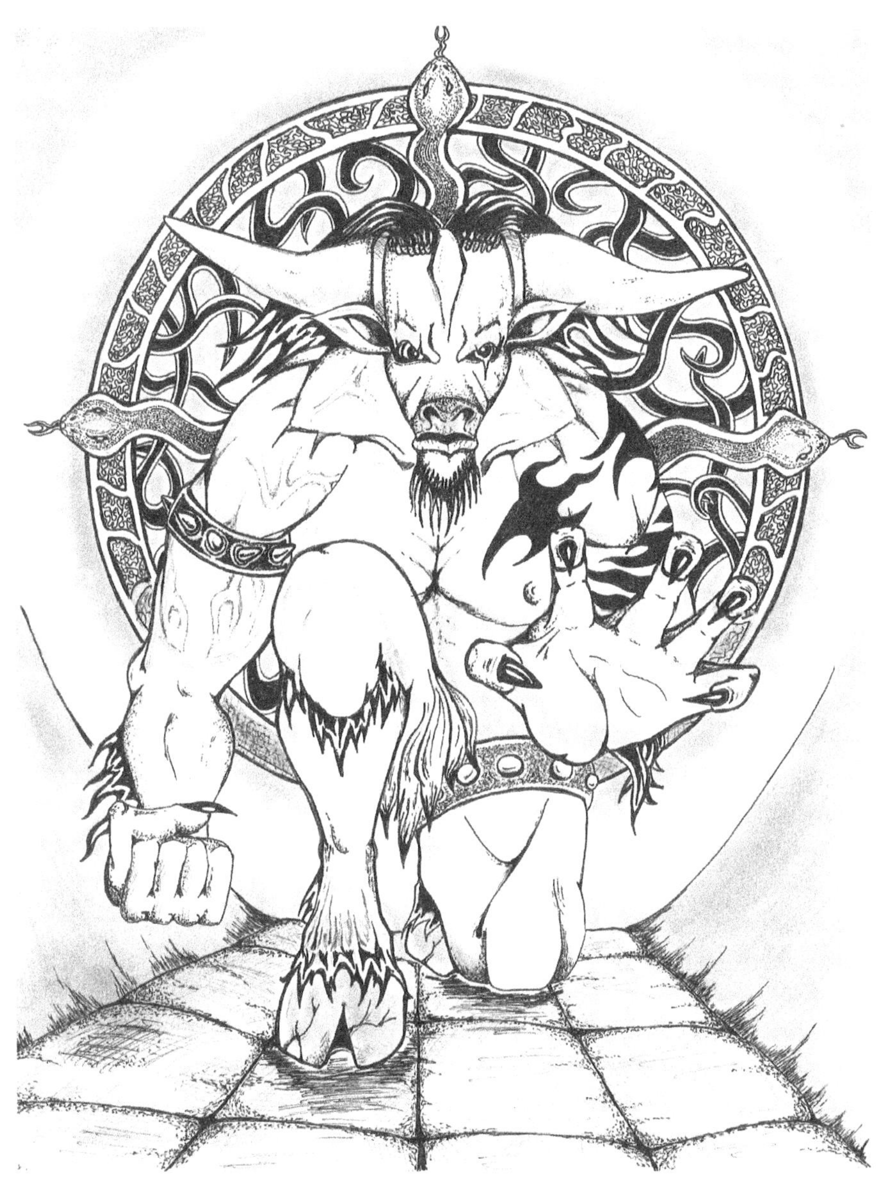

Little-Lost Jewel

(An ode to her night without armor)

I consume your thoughts
and inside me they find home
a place to rest

Nothing so potent as understanding
to ward away a cold night
or a song too often played
or a lonely room of strangers pretending to be friends

Feeling lost together binds me to the paintings of your mind
Their familiarity speaks to me
inspiring me to find you

But I could never keep you to myself
I would not want to
Such beautifully rationed pain must be shared
for hidden words have little value

But allowing others to stare at your facets
to hold you up to the light
is a form of nakedness

And so, as your thoughts wander from hand to hand
slipping through grasping fingers
I hope you find the peace you gave me
knowing there are those who understood you

P.S. "Little" is not a diminutive term,
but rather a measure of degree: As in "not very"

A Sadness

Today the sky turned gray, today it rained.
It rained for me.
Weeping for my lost shine,
for eyes too stained, too sordid.
Today I count the falling sky as a friend.

This cold October wind
is far easier to bear than the coming pain.
I am already worn out,
yet I must still endure being torn down,
stripped,
wasted.
And I am afraid.

For a brief moment an angel appears.
Offering succor in the form of a warm touch,
a vanilla scent
and red fire.
But she could not stay.
Her wings too soft to lift my burden entirely.
And as her light fades,
I turn my face once more towards the wind,
and embrace the rain.

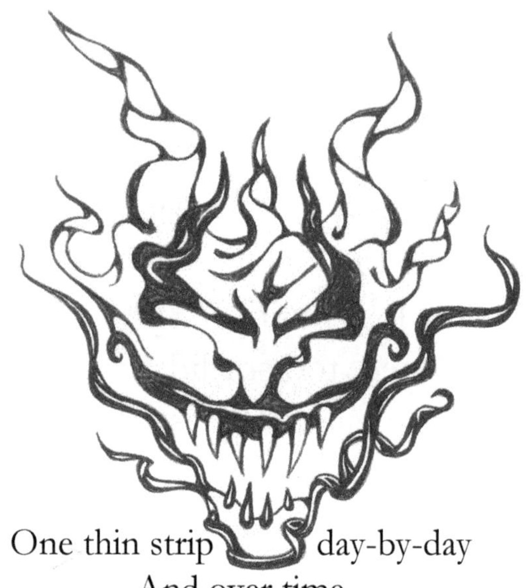

One thin strip day-by-day
And over time
I will bind you with
PAPER CHAINS

Paper Chains
So easily broken by a simple act of will
So Light
They're a burden almost impossible to feel
No Scars
no one knows and none can see
The Paper Demon
is it really even haunting me
A Sweet Dilemma
Why turn nothing into a fight
You Can't Endure
when the longing comes again tonight

A Night of Firsts

It was a shared night of carefree laughter
A mixed drink of companionship and vanilla Coke
More elegant our mood than our plastic cup toast

I'm glad you were brave enough to climb with me
It allowed Spring to reflect in the green of your eyes
Like watching new flowers feel the warmth of the sun
for the first time

My practiced smooth confidence
betrayed by a tremble
I love that you noticed

Were I not so intrigued, my kiss would have been less
awkward
(I'm only that clumsy when I'm truly interested)
I hope I can regain my composure
before our second date

<u>The Fool's Journal:</u> Doorway 6 - The Toppled Lovers

How could I have ever told you no?
You certainly loved the hunt
and everything that followed
Your timing – perfect
I could feel your eyes through the phone
Danger, anticipation, but the guilt is all your own
Our flavors blur as our bodies entwine
I know what makes you feel the aftershocks
and you know what makes me pine
Forbidden flesh writhing on the floor
A union neither should partake
Yet we both came back for more
You were the one place that I had never been
And after you
will prob'ly never be again

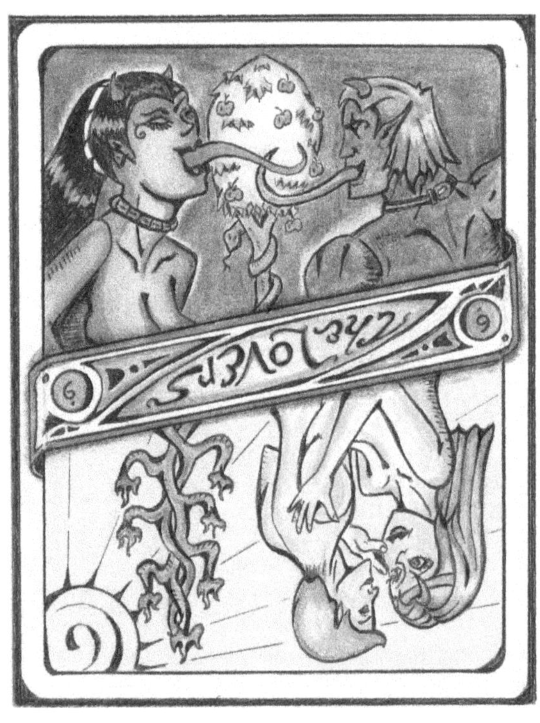

Intoxicate

The light caress of my breath on your neck tingles so intensely that you arch your back happily; but involuntarily.
My hands' slow march from your hip upwards, slides under your shirt, across your bare skin, finally nudging the soft curve of your breast.
Your hands, tangled in my hair, jump to my waist - insuring that there is as little space between us as possible - and the pressure makes both of us vocalize our pleasure.

-Kissing, Touching, Feeling –
The heat builds, as does our impatience to tear off clothing.

The silky warmth of skin on skin makes us drunk. And as I lift you from the floor, your legs instinctively wrap around my back - holding me as if molded to fit.
As I carry you to bed, our pitch becomes more fevered. The more we touch, the more we want, and quickly we lose our individuality.
All other existence ceases, there is nothing and no one else but you and I. Even time is suspended – or at least, we are heedless of it.
Our embrace grows ever tighter, our breathing more inconsistent. But right now, air is of secondary importance.

-The sweetest taste comes from being with you-
And then, suddenly, our time as gods is over.

The pace slows and our eyes lock. No words are necessary, your smile is enough. You collapse into my shoulder and my arms encircle your shape as I lightly stroke your cheek.
Before drifting off to sleep, you lick the sweat off your lips. You smile, knowing that the experience will soon be repeated.
You can hardly wait to wake up again.

The Good Wall

The softest breeze blows,
and the branches of the slender Aspen rock lightly to the natural rhythm.
Within the security of the leaves
I find myself atop the capstone of a gray brick wall.
This is where I come to sit, to rest, to ponder.
I am young, unaware, and the wall provides stability.
I remember the time before the wall.
I remember being upset while helping construct it.
At the time it represented restriction.
But as my sweat dripped from my face, mingling with the mortar,
I became a part of it.
Now, perched atop, encircled by the emerald leaves,
I am shielded from heavy eyes.
Here my thoughts and dreams can bathe in the sunshine
yet still not be compromised.
No contamination from voices, ideas, and minds,
that are not mine.
There on my wall, lounging like a cat,
I am as calm as the breeze that carries the scent of lilac to my senses.
Making memories.
Stock piling them against the coming winter's sting.
Amazingly, I get all that, from sitting on a wall.

Fate's a Bitch

I shake my fists at the gods and scream:
"I am not your plaything!"
But no matter the violence I bring into being,
no matter how tightly I grit my teeth,
it still doesn't change my stars.
- So I change my tactics -
I bow down and then begin to pray:
"Please stop treating me this way."
But no matter how deeply I bend my knees,
no matter how fervent I make my pleas,
my doom remains the same.
- So I change my tactics -
I get to work, toil day-and-night:
"I'll do it myself, I'll change my own plight!"
But no matter how much sweat I spill,
no matter the force of my diligent will,
things still don't go my way.
- So I change my tactics -
I end my striving and quietly say:
"I think it's time to accept my fate."
While recurring failures still menace me,
from frustration's strife I am not set free,
I seem to suffer less.

The Pebble

A pebble bounces along in a fast moving stream.
As I watch it tumble by, I wonder:
Does it resent all the bumps?
Is it jealous of the larger stones?
Does it feel small as it crashes into their majestic stability?
Or, is it just a pebble?
Quietly fulfilling the measure of its creation.
Completely unaware of its plight.

If only I could fill my role in the grander scheme with such quiet dignity,
without complaint.
But I resent the forces that knock me around,
wearing me down into sand.

Happy Shackles

Today while stuck in traffic
I saw the most beautiful woman in a Mercedes sitting next to me.
It wasn't until she removed her sunglasses,
to wipe a tear from her eye,
that I noticed she'd been crying.

Aren't we the fools -
Masking our emotions from one another
with makeup, Gucci, and big houses.
Burying ourselves beneath layers of finely woven cloth,
meant to show others how happy we are.
In this aspect, I almost admire the "freaks"…
The street people, the Goths, the Punk Rockers.
At least their clothes reflect the truth of their discontent.
Even if it's more about rebellion than a deliberate choice.

We spend mountains of money,
to build a tiny mound of ego.
And then we defend it like it was a priceless treasure.
I guess if you measure value by cost,
you would see this illusion as a treasure.
Sure it cost you your money;
but are you sure it didn't also cost you your soul?

BETRAYAL

Precious and fragile
A friend entrusted to me the care
of a beautiful crystal angel

Priceless in value
yet in my careless folly
I broke her delicate wings

There are no words
No words to convey my sorrow
No words that can heal the wound

There is not enough glue
not enough in the entire world
to mend a broken trust

The Crocodile's Rules

The predator that most haunts you
is the one that preys unseen
if you play in the murky waters of the world
you're playing by the crocodile's rules

You pay Big Brother to watch
give them power to govern you and me
Discretion as they see fit, for security & efficiency
But in the murky waters of public trust
You're playing by the crocodile's rules

The economy is booming, keep the cash-cow fed
A new Visa offer every day
They told you your credit was endless… you believed them
But in the murky waters of finance
You're playing by the crocodile's rules

Refinance, bankruptcy, world politics
Giant corporations, drinking habits
Keep watching the NEWS they'll tell you how to proceed
No disinformation comes across your TV

But on this muddy turf, the crocodiles rule

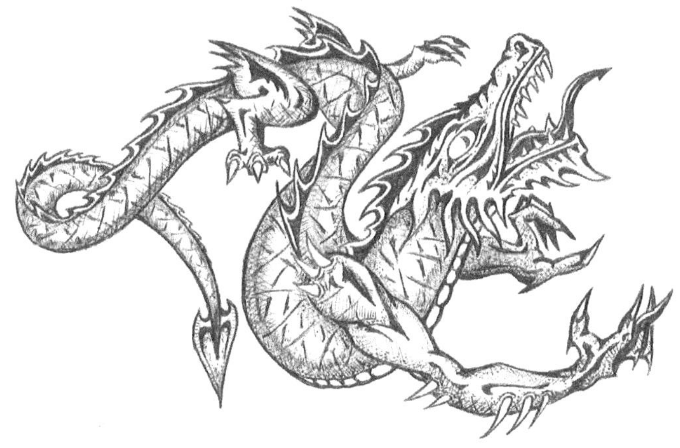

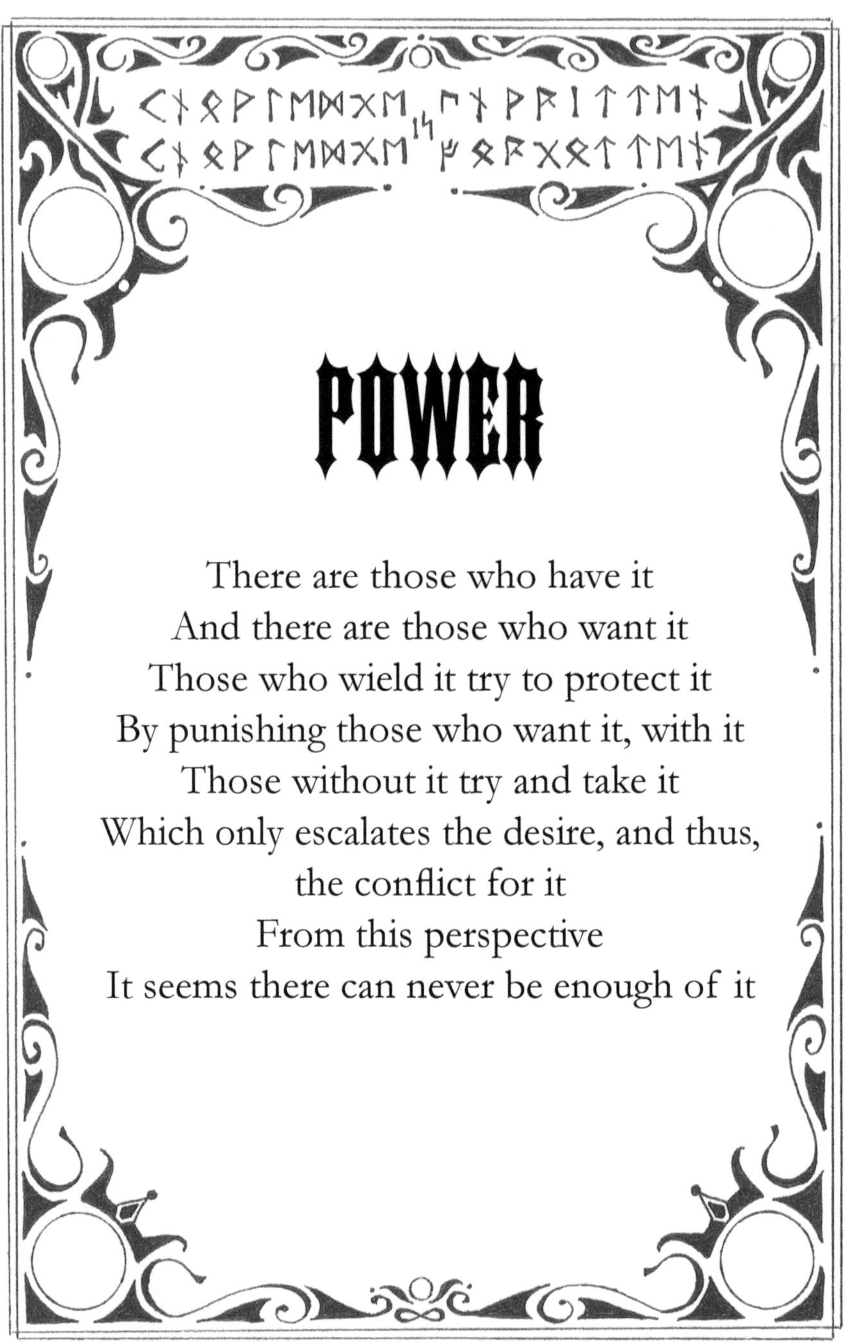

POWER

There are those who have it
And there are those who want it
Those who wield it try to protect it
By punishing those who want it, with it
Those without it try and take it
Which only escalates the desire, and thus,
the conflict for it
From this perspective
It seems there can never be enough of it

The Hardest Lesson in Highschool

I feel like the product of someone else's fantasy.
I dress in their fashions,
I use their examples,
I walk and talk in the accepted way of the day.
I also attend their schools,
where I learn even more about how to become someone else.
Don't misunderstand,
I recognize the need for a basic outline for society to exist.
But this feels more like a final draft.
It's ironic:
The theme of my generation *"different is good"*
had us all rushing to the closest store
to buy the things we needed to be different:
Attractively packaged of course.
But what if I didn't want all that stuff?
Which, oddly enough, was different.
Was I applauded for my individuality? - No –
Instead, I found animosity, ridicule, and scorn.
Confused, I decided to conform.
And once I obtained the difference that others had in mind for me,
I was accepted.
Everyone told me to be myself.
They just didn't tell me I had to do it their way.

Wanderlust
(in the key of D)

V.1- Driving in my car, going down the same 'ole road,
I see an open highway, and I wonder where it goes.
Got a full tank of gas, should I try something new?
I question all I've ever known and decide what to do.

Ch.1- My tires squeal as I make the turn.
What's on the horizon? I'm dying to learn.
Will I crash? Will my engine blow?
I can't wait to see where this goes.

V.2- I'm seeing brand new sights, and I'm breathing brand new air.
The uncertainty of freedom is blow'n through my hair.
I make a stop for gas, and I see you in those jeans.
You wink in my direction and I know what it means.

Ch.2- I'm headed for nowhere and moving fast.
You ask can you join me, though you know it won't last.
Eyes bright as you climb in, our wanderlust grows.
We can't wait to see where this goes.

Ch.3- We ran like the wolves into midnight air.
We held nothin' back; it's a life so rare.
We flew just for fun like the ravens and crows,
yeah we got to see where it goes.

V.3- Now I look back on that life, and I wouldn't change a thing.
Running unknown highways to live a life of dreams.
I saw you yesterday, still look'n good in jeans.
You were walking with your family, and I know what it means…

Ch.4- Your wander days over, you've settled at last.
There's only so long you can live life so fast.
The summer of life always ends with the snow,
but we got to see where it goes.

V.4- And so I traveled on, I too have found a home.
But I smile at the highway, 'cuz I know where it goes.

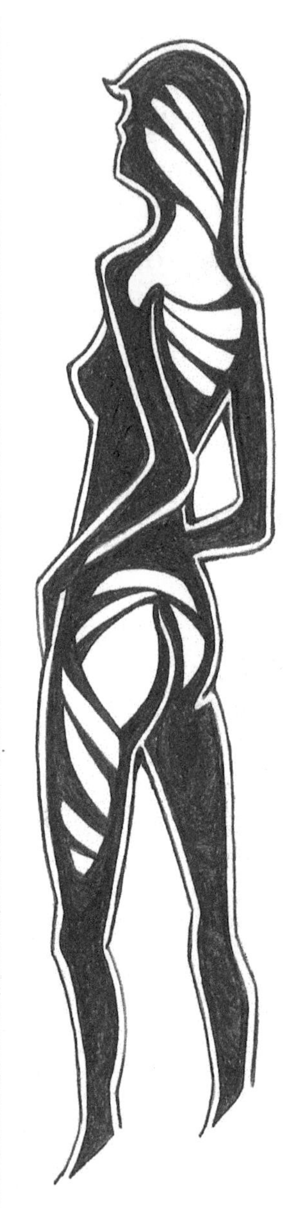

Dancing Eyes

Perfect tiny urban dancer,
who's the lucky one?
Who knows your name - your true name?

And when his hands caress you,
do they brush away all the eyes
that on your soft skin stayed stuck?

Or, is he a she with whom you find comfort?
Making me twice as jealous,
and possibly less of a man

-Or-
My perfect tiny dancer
are you alone like me?
Curling up with only a pillow when you sleep.
Remembering all the eyes you've seen,
watching you intimately.

Making, but not sharing, dreams

ROCKET
(in the key of G)

V.1- Some will want to stay within their beds,
safe and warm while waiting for their deaths.
But I'm the type who likes to surge ahead.
This is how I roll…

V.2- Bullet-bikes a hundred miles an hour,
and triple-flips from off the bungee tower,
I'll quit when I'm push'n up the flowers,
That's how I wanna go… yeah that's how I wanna go!

Ch.- I know the curves of every fallen angel
And I've felt the pain of sleep'n all alone
But I'm not the type to run away from danger…
a rocket ship is tattooed on my soul

Br.1- And that's how I wanna go-oh-oh-oh
That's how I wanna go
Burn hot, fly'n low - that's how I wanna go!
Can't live move'n slow, that's not the way to go
No rules to follow - That's how I wanna go
That's how I wanna go
That's how I wanna go-oh

V.3- Parachutes for jumping out of planes,
make me laugh, but you don't think I'm sane.
Girls are always call'n out my name,
and I like how that goes…

V.4- So while you're sleep'n in your bed tonight,
I'll be out to pick another fight.
I'll die young but dying young's alright.
This is the life I chose… This is the life I chose!

Ch.- I know the curves of every fallen angel
And I've felt the pain of sleep'n all alone
But I'm not the type to run away from danger…
a rocket ship is tattooed on my soul

Br.1- And that's how I wanna go-oh-oh-oh
That's how I wanna go
Burn hot, fly'n low - That's how I wanna go

Br.2- They want you to follow, to steal your tomorrow.
They'll put you in line but they can't make you stay!

Br.1- Whoa-oh-oh-oh here's how I wanna go
Burn hot, fly'n low - That's how I wanna go
Can't live mov'n slow, that's not the way to go
No rules to follow - That's how I wanna go
That's how I wanna go
That's how I wanna go-oh…
-That's how I wanna go!-

Outro- (with audience) Oh, oh, oh, I'm a rocket let me fly…(repeat as necessary)

Spiral

V.1- The Lady's call it beckons me
In midnight wood she sets me free
Like new blood running through my veins
The magic of that night remains

Ch.1- The seasons change and so must I
From Summer's heat, the Fall leaves fly
From Winter's grip, to Spring's renew
There are those who cannot see - but I do

V.2- I wandered paths that were strange to me
What might-have-been, what should I be
The Hunter called, I heard his voice
He said I always have a choice

Ch.1- The seasons change and so must I
From Summer's heat, the Fall leaves fly
From Winter's grip, to Spring's renew
There are those who cannot see - but I do

Br.1- (Spoken, not sung)
The Wind will blow, the Earth will stand
Fire and Water, they shape the land
The Maker's gift: There's so much we can choose

V.3- I felt the call of passion young
The sweet night air, it filled my lungs
The panpipes whispered on the breeze
A wolf's heart born beneath the trees

Ch.1- The seasons change and so must I
From Summer's heat, the Fall leaves fly
From Winter's grip, to Spring's renew
There are those who cannot see - but I do

V.4- Bodies move in rhythmic time
The cycles of our lives unwind
The circle brings us 'round again
The spiral makes our lives deepen

Ch.2- The seasons changed and so did I
The Gods have watched as time goes by
The breath of life, my soul renewed
There are those who cannot see - but I do

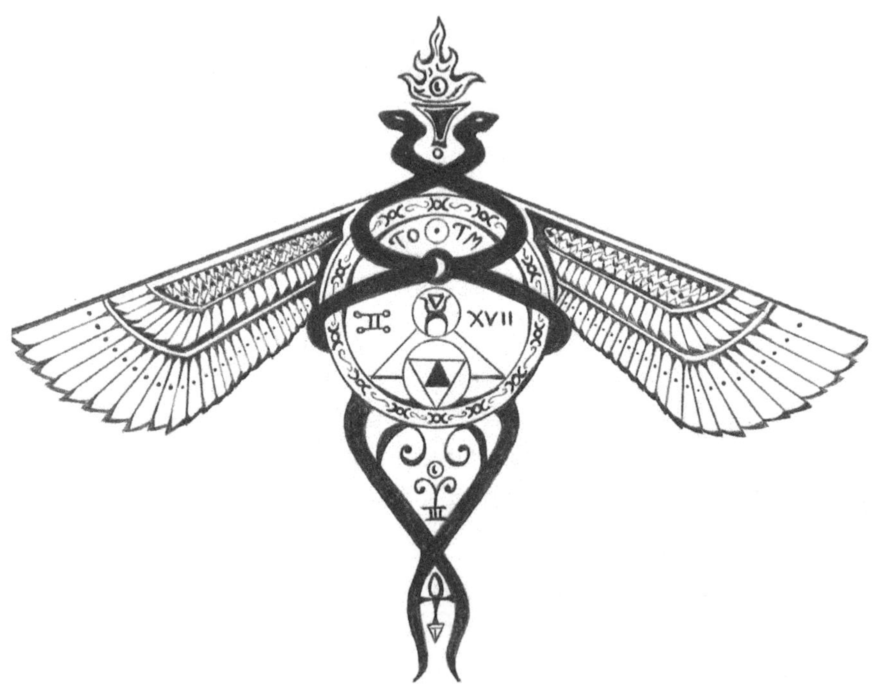

Brick by Brick

Brick by brick each life is built, but what's very seldom known, the reason why each brick was laid, and its effect upon the whole.
When we gaze at human beings, the entirety of each life,
we cannot tell from this wide view, the "why" for our dislike.
We only see a wall that's bowed, or a building less-than-grand,
but without the story of each brick, we cannot understand.
Perhaps some ugly twist of fate, caused important bricks to crack, and if not for luck and effort, that whole life would have collapsed.
Thin mortar mixed in poverty, or a chain of family traits,
manufactured bricks too weak to hold this life and all its weight.
But once we know the reason why a foundation wasn't straight,
we judge anew, and this is true, up close it's hard to hate.

<u>The Fool`s Journal:</u> Entry W-6: Nostalgia

The strings of my guitar used to hum.
But even that connection to humanity was stolen.
Like so many other things I deeply love…
        -Loved-
It seems that whenever I truly care about something,
it always ends up in the past tense.

My UA Cup

(Sung to the tune of Toby Keith's "Red Solo Cup ")
-A tribute to the Prison's drug testing policy-

V.1- Now, I really hate how they wake me in the morning
And pull me away from my cell-mate's heavy snoring
To walk down the hall without any warning
Just so I can pee in a cup

V.2- They smile when they ask if my meds are all sanctioned
What they really wanna know, have I been drinking libations
made from toilet wine and some cheeked medications
and then they take a peek at my junk.

Chorus(x2)- My UA Cup, I fill you up
Let's see if you partied
Did you have a party?

V.3- So I never understood why in a free country
you don't have the right to bake weed in your munchies
nor why my getting high would make you so grumpy
But your judgement's really harsh`n my buzz

V.4- Well you know that there's millions who like smok`n ganja
and not just on weekends, but whenever they wanna
So, when the feds legalize home-grown marijuana
Then you can stick this cup in yer butt

Chorus(x2)- My UA Cup, I fill you up
Let's see if you partied
Did you have a party?

V.5- What an auspicious start to my latest birthday
When a voice on a com yells- "You've got a U.A."
It'll be less of a problem as I reach old age
With incontinence I'll just hand them my pants

Chorus(x2)- My UA Cup, I fill you up
Let's see if you partied
Did you have a party?

THE LEGEND OF TOMMY TWO-GUNS
(in A minor)

V.1- Young Tommy Tew he was a boy, for him this life it held no joy
`till the devil put two guns into his hands
He smelt the powder, he felt the steel, 'till then his life had not been real
And he screamed into the sky… "I feel alive!"

Br.1- From town to town he made his name
His guns rang out and filled the graves
And many mothers cried for their sons
With blackened heart and one-by-one
He carved the notches in his guns
And you could hear him cry… "I feel alive!" "I feel alive!"

V.2- Quick fingers played a deadly dirge, the bullets flew, the bodies lurched
His thunder cut the air just like a knife
And even in the cities tall, hard men lined up only to fall
His guns they never failed, he killed them all.

Br.2- And then one day a lawman came
To send poor Tommy to his grave
They drew at twenty paces and cut loose
When the smoke had cleared there was just one man
Who stood with two guns in his hands
And Tommy's cry rang high… "I'm still alive!" "I'm still alive!"

V.3- So he strapped his pistols into place, he'd live to fight another day
But he knew he had to get out of this town
As he turned to leave that fateful place, behind him stood a pretty face
It was the lawman's wife who stared him down

Br.3- Her eyes were wild, they held the fire
Of hell and all her lost desires
And they burned like the six-gun in her hand
The hammer fell, the powder flashed
The bullet ripped, and his eyes rolled back
And Tommy Two-guns faded into black…into the black

-Sorrowful Instrumental Interlude-

V.4- But if you think our story ends, you don't know Tommy well my friends
'cuz death for one like him's a two-way door
And out on lonesome prairie night, you'll hear his thunder & ghostly cries
ring-out forever more…"I'm still alive!" "I'm still alive!"

A Prayer for a Change

Yours are the twin pillars whose rescue I seek
From the chains of the Hierophant's dark slavery
Reveal to me what mortal eyes fail to see
I'd kill reason to swim in your depths

Your gifts may be more than I'd understand
My foundation was built on this world's shifting sands
Let your mysteries teach, let me travel your lands
I'd drink deeply from all of its flavors

The path that once bore me is a grand puppet show
I played my part poorly their stage swallowed me whole
Let your waters reveal all that I need to know
Beyond sense let me sail the uncertain

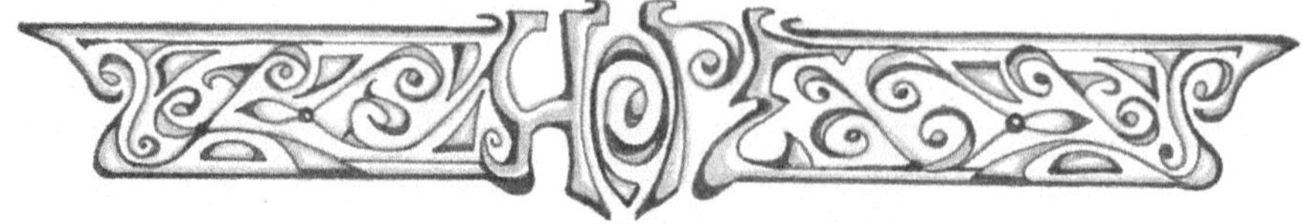

Hope is something unique
It can never be destroyed - only lost
And that gives you hope of finding it again
And that is Hope

Hope is not "real"
But it is always there for you to hold onto
And that is Hope

Hope is everyone's future
For there is nothing in the future
that cannot be described as being hoped for
And that is Hope

Hope is everyone's past
For all the regrets of your past
are things you hope never to repeat
And that is Hope

Every prayer is a hope to be heard
Every tear is a hope to be healed
Every seed planted
is a hope to never be left with nothing
But even if life takes everything, dashing your hopes and dreams
it can't take away your hope of rebuilding
And that is Hope

Yes, Hope is something unique
All you have to do is think about it, and it appears
Isn't that something!
And that is Hope

www.ingramcontent.com/pod-product-compliance
Ingram Content Group UK Ltd.
Pitfield, Milton Keynes, MK11 3LW, UK
UKHW020140250726
13967UKWH00002B/767